CW01276950

JUST A …IRL WHO LOVES

PANDAS

THIS JOURNAL BELONGS TO

JUST A GIRL
WHO LOVES
PANDAS

JUST A GIRL
WHO LOVES
PANDAS

JUST A GIRL
WHO LOVES
PANDAS

JUST A GIRL
WHO LOVES
PANDAS

JUST A GIRL
WHO LOVES
PANDAS

JUST A GIRL
WHO LOVES
PANDAS

JUST A GIRL
WHO LOVES
PANDAS

JUST A GIRL
WHO LOVES
PANDAS

JUST A GIRL
WHO LOVES
PANDAS

JUST A GIRL
WHO LOVES
PANDAS

JUST A GIRL
WHO LOVES
PANDAS

JUST A GIRL
WHO LOVES
PANDAS

JUST A GIRL
WHO LOVES
PANDAS

JUST A GIRL
WHO LOVES
PANDAS

JUST A GIRL
WHO LOVES
PANDAS

JUST A GIRL
WHO LOVES
PANDAS

JUST A GIRL
WHO LOVES
PANDAS

JUST A GIRL
WHO LOVES
PANDAS

JUST A GIRL
WHO LOVES
PANDAS

JUST A GIRL
WHO LOVES
PANDAS

JUST A GIRL
WHO LOVES
PANDAS

JUST A GIRL
WHO LOVES
PANDAS

JUST A GIRL
WHO LOVES
PANDAS

JUST A GIRL
WHO LOVES
PANDAS

JUST A GIRL
WHO LOVES
PANDAS

JUST A GIRL
WHO LOVES
PANDAS

JUST A GIRL
WHO LOVES
PANDAS

JUST A GIRL
WHO LOVES
PANDAS

JUST A GIRL
WHO LOVES
PANDAS

JUST A GIRL
WHO LOVES
PANDAS

JUST A GIRL
WHO LOVES
PANDAS

JUST A GIRL
WHO LOVES
PANDAS

JUST A GIRL
WHO LOVES
PANDAS

JUST A GIRL
WHO LOVES
PANDAS

JUST A GIRL
WHO LOVES
PANDAS

JUST A GIRL
WHO LOVES
PANDAS

JUST A GIRL
WHO LOVES
PANDAS

JUST A GIRL
WHO LOVES
PANDAS

JUST A GIRL
WHO LOVES
PANDAS

JUST A GIRL
WHO LOVES
PANDAS

JUST A GIRL
WHO LOVES
PANDAS

JUST A GIRL
WHO LOVES
PANDAS

JUST A GIRL
WHO LOVES
PANDAS

JUST A GIRL
WHO LOVES
PANDAS

JUST A GIRL
WHO LOVES
PANDAS

JUST A GIRL
WHO LOVES
PANDAS

JUST A GIRL
WHO LOVES
PANDAS

JUST A GIRL
WHO LOVES
PANDAS

JUST A GIRL
WHO LOVES
PANDAS

JUST A GIRL
WHO LOVES
PANDAS

JUST A GIRL
WHO LOVES
PANDAS

JUST A GIRL
WHO LOVES
PANDAS

JUST A GIRL
WHO LOVES
PANDAS

JUST A GIRL
WHO LOVES
PANDAS

Printed in Great Britain
by Amazon

70918853R00066